This Journal belongs To:

_____

Project Name: _____

Start Date: _____

Sewing Pattern: _____

End Date: _____

Supplies

- ☐ ....
- ☐ ....
- ☐ ....
- ☐ ....
- ☐ ....
- ☐ ....
- ☐ ....
- ☐ ....
- ☐ ....

Sketch:

Thread Used: _____

Needle Used: _____

Sewing Machine Settings:

Stitch Length:

Stitch Width:

Stitch Tension:

Main Fabric Sample:

Lining Fabric Sample:

Notes:

....

....

....

....

....

....

....

....

Interfacing Sample:

How was it ?

◯ ◯ ◯ ◯
Bad   Mhh,Ok   Liked it   Loved it!

Difficulty: ◯ ◯ ◯ ◯

Will I make it again ? ☐ Yes ☐ No

What went well:

....
....
....
....
....
....

What was difficult:

....
....
....
....
....
....

Changes I made to the original pattern:

Notes to my future self:

....
....
....
....
....
....

Project Name:

Start Date:

Sewing Pattern:

End Date:

Supplies

- [ ] ....
- [ ] ....
- [ ] ....
- [ ] ....
- [ ] ....
- [ ] ....
- [ ] ....
- [ ] ....
- [ ] ....

Sketch:

Thread Used:

Needle Used:

Sewing Machine Settings:

Stitch Length:

Stitch Width:

Stitch Tension:

Main Fabric Sample:

Lining Fabric Sample:

Notes:

....

....

....

....

....

....

....

Interfacing Sample:

How was it ?

○ ○ ○ ○
Bad Mhh,Ok Liked it Loved it!

Difficulty: ○ ○ ○ ○

Will I make it again ? ☐ Yes ☐ No

What went well:

....

....

....

....

....

....

What was difficult:

....

....

....

....

....

....

Changes I made to the original pattern:

Notes to my future self:

....

....

....

....

....

....

Project Name:

Start Date:

Sewing Pattern:

End Date:

Supplies

- ☐ ....
- ☐ ....
- ☐ ....
- ☐ ....
- ☐ ....
- ☐ ....
- ☐ ....
- ☐ ....
- ☐ ....

Sketch:

Thread Used:

Needle Used:

Sewing Machine Settings:

Stitch Length:

Stitch Width:

Stitch Tension:

Main Fabric Sample:

Lining Fabric Sample:

Notes:

....
....
....
....
....
....
....
....

Interfacing Sample:

How was it ?

○ ○ ○ ○
Bad   Mhh,Ok   Liked it   Loved it!

Difficulty: ○ ○ ○ ○

Will I make it again ? ☐ Yes ☐ No

What went well:

....
....
....
....
....
....

What was difficult:

....
....
....
....
....
....

Changes I made to the original pattern:

Notes to my future self:

....
....
....
....
....
....

Project Name:

Start Date:

Sewing Pattern:

End Date:

Supplies

- [ ] ....
- [ ] ....
- [ ] ....
- [ ] ....
- [ ] ....
- [ ] ....
- [ ] ....
- [ ] ....
- [ ] ....

Thread Used:

Needle Used:

Sewing Machine Settings:
Stitch Length:
Stitch Width:
Stitch Tension:

Notes:

....
....
....
....
....
....
....
....

Sketch:

Main Fabric Sample:

Lining Fabric Sample:

Interfacing Sample:

How was it ?

○ ○ ○ ○
Bad   Mhh,Ok   Liked it   Loved it!

Difficulty: ○ ○ ○ ○

Will I make it again ? ☐ Yes ☐ No

What went well:

....
....
....
....
....
....

What was difficult:

....
....
....
....
....
....

Changes I made to the original pattern:

Notes to my future self:

....
....
....
....
....
....

Project Name:

Start Date:

Sewing Pattern:

End Date:

Supplies

- [ ] ....
- [ ] ....
- [ ] ....
- [ ] ....
- [ ] ....
- [ ] ....
- [ ] ....
- [ ] ....
- [ ] ....

Sketch:

Thread Used:

Needle Used:

Sewing Machine Settings:

Stitch Length:

Stitch Width:

Stitch Tension:

Main Fabric Sample:

Lining Fabric Sample:

Notes:

....

....

....

....

....

....

....

Interfacing Sample:

How was it ?

○ ○ ○ ○
Bad   Mhh,Ok   Liked it   Loved it!

Difficulty: ○ ○ ○ ○

Will I make it again ? ☐ Yes ☐ No

What went well:

....
....
....
....
....
....

What was difficult:

....
....
....
....
....
....

Changes I made to the original pattern:

Notes to my future self:

....
....
....
....
....
....

Project Name:

Start Date:

Sewing Pattern:

End Date:

Supplies

☐ ....
☐ ....
☐ ....
☐ ....
☐ ....
☐ ....
☐ ....
☐ ....
☐ ....

Sketch:

Thread Used:

Needle Used:

Sewing Machine Settings:

Stitch Length:

Stitch Width:

Stitch Tension:

Main Fabric Sample:

Lining Fabric Sample:

Notes:

....
....
....
....
....
....
....
....

Interfacing Sample:

How was it ?

○ ○ ○ ○
Bad   Mhh,Ok   Liked it   Loved it!

Difficulty: ○ ○ ○ ○

Will I make it again ? ☐ Yes ☐ No

What went well:

....
....
....
....
....
....

What was difficult:

....
....
....
....
....
....

Changes I made to the original pattern:

Notes to my future self:

....
....
....
....
....
....

Project Name: _____

Start Date: _____

Sewing Pattern: _____

End Date: _____

Supplies

- ☐ ....
- ☐ ....
- ☐ ....
- ☐ ....
- ☐ ....
- ☐ ....
- ☐ ....
- ☐ ....
- ☐ ....

Sketch:

Thread Used: _____

Needle Used: _____

Sewing Machine Settings:

Stitch Length:

Stitch Width:

Stitch Tension:

Main Fabric Sample: _____

Lining Fabric Sample: _____

Notes:

....
....
....
....
....
....
....

Interfacing Sample:

How was it ?

◯ ◯ ◯ ◯
Bad Mhh,Ok Liked it Loved it!

Difficulty: ◯ ◯ ◯ ◯

Will I make it again ? ☐ Yes ☐ No

What went well:

....
....
....
....
....
....

What was difficult:

....
....
....
....
....
....

Changes I made to the original pattern:

Notes to my future self:

....
....
....
....
....
....

Project Name: _____

Start Date: _____

Sewing Pattern: _____

End Date: _____

Supplies

- ☐ _____
- ☐ _____
- ☐ _____
- ☐ _____
- ☐ _____
- ☐ _____
- ☐ _____
- ☐ _____
- ☐ _____

Sketch:

Thread Used: _____

Needle Used: _____

Sewing Machine Settings:

Stitch Length:

Stitch Width:

Stitch Tension:

Main Fabric Sample: _____

Lining Fabric Sample: _____

Interfacing Sample: _____

Notes:

_____

_____

_____

_____

_____

_____

_____

How was it ?

○ ○ ○ ○
Bad   Mhh,Ok   Liked it   Loved it!

Difficulty:

○ ○ ○ ○

Will I make it again ? ☐ Yes ☐ No

What went well:

....

....

....

....

....

....

What was difficult:

....

....

....

....

....

....

Changes I made to the original pattern:

Notes to my future self:

....

....

....

....

....

....

Project Name:

Start Date:

Sewing Pattern:

End Date:

Supplies

- [ ] ....
- [ ] ....
- [ ] ....
- [ ] ....
- [ ] ....
- [ ] ....
- [ ] ....
- [ ] ....
- [ ] ....

Sketch:

Thread Used:

Needle Used:

Sewing Machine Settings:

Stitch Length:

Stitch Width:

Stitch Tension:

Main Fabric Sample:

Lining Fabric Sample:

Notes:

....
....
....
....
....
....
....

Interfacing Sample:

How was it ?

◯ ◯ ◯ ◯
Bad   Mhh,Ok   Liked it   Loved it!

Difficulty: ◯ ◯ ◯ ◯

Will I make it again ? ☐ Yes ☐ No

What went well:

....
....
....
....
....
....

What was difficult:

....
....
....
....
....
....

Changes I made to the original pattern:

Notes to my future self:

....
....
....
....
....
....

Project Name: _____ Start Date: _____

Sewing Pattern: _____ End Date: _____

Supplies

☐ ....
☐ ....
☐ ....
☐ ....
☐ ....
☐ ....
☐ ....
☐ ....
☐ ....

Thread Used: _____

Needle Used: _____

Sewing Machine Settings:
Stitch Length:
Stitch Width:
Stitch Tension:

Notes:

....
....
....
....
....
....
....

Sketch:

Main Fabric Sample: _____

Lining Fabric Sample: _____

Interfacing Sample: _____

How was it ?

◯ ◯ ◯ ◯
Bad Mhh,Ok Liked it Loved it!

Difficulty: ◯ ◯ ◯ ◯

Will I make it again ? ☐ Yes ☐ No

What went well:

....
....
....
....
....
....
....

What was difficult:

....
....
....
....
....
....
....

Changes I made to the original pattern:

Notes to my future self:

....
....
....
....
....
....

Project Name:

Start Date:

Sewing Pattern:

End Date:

Supplies

- [ ] ....
- [ ] ....
- [ ] ....
- [ ] ....
- [ ] ....
- [ ] ....
- [ ] ....
- [ ] ....
- [ ] ....

Sketch:

Thread Used:

Needle Used:

Sewing Machine Settings:

Stitch Length:

Stitch Width:

Stitch Tension:

Main Fabric Sample:

Lining Fabric Sample:

Notes:

....

....

....

....

....

....

....

Interfacing Sample:

How was it ?

○ ○ ○ ○
Bad Mhh,Ok Liked it Loved it!

Difficulty: ○ ○ ○ ○

Will I make it again ? ☐ Yes ☐ No

What went well:

....
....
....
....
....
....

What was difficult:

....
....
....
....
....
....

Changes I made to the original pattern:

Notes to my future self:

....
....
....
....
....
....

Project Name:

Start Date:

Sewing Pattern:

End Date:

Supplies

- [ ] ....
- [ ] ....
- [ ] ....
- [ ] ....
- [ ] ....
- [ ] ....
- [ ] ....
- [ ] ....
- [ ] ....

Sketch:

Thread Used:

Needle Used:

Sewing Machine Settings:

Stitch Length:

Stitch Width:

Stitch Tension:

Main Fabric Sample:

Lining Fabric Sample:

Notes:

....

....

....

....

....

....

....

Interfacing Sample:

How was it ?
○ ○ ○ ○
Bad   Mhh,Ok   Liked it   Loved it!

Difficulty: ○ ○ ○ ○

Will I make it again ? ☐ Yes ☐ No

What went well:

....
....
....
....
....
....

What was difficult:

....
....
....
....
....
....

Changes I made to the original pattern:

Notes to my future self:

....
....
....
....
....
....

Project Name: _____

Start Date: _____

Sewing Pattern: _____

End Date: _____

Supplies

- [ ] _____
- [ ] _____
- [ ] _____
- [ ] _____
- [ ] _____
- [ ] _____
- [ ] _____
- [ ] _____
- [ ] _____

Sketch:

Thread Used: _____

Needle Used: _____

Sewing Machine Settings:

Stitch Length:

Stitch Width:

Stitch Tension:

Main Fabric Sample: _____

Lining Fabric Sample: _____

Interfacing Sample: _____

Notes:

_____

_____

_____

_____

_____

_____

_____

How was it ?

Bad   Mhh,Ok   Liked it   Loved it!

Difficulty: ◯ ◯ ◯ ◯

Will I make it again ? ☐ Yes ☐ No

What went well:

What was difficult:

Changes I made to the original pattern:

Notes to my future self:

Project Name: _____

Start Date: _____

Sewing Pattern: _____

End Date: _____

Supplies

- ☐ ....
- ☐ ....
- ☐ ....
- ☐ ....
- ☐ ....
- ☐ ....
- ☐ ....
- ☐ ....
- ☐ ....

Sketch:

Thread Used: _____

Needle Used: _____

Sewing Machine Settings:

Stitch Length:

Stitch Width:

Stitch Tension:

Main Fabric Sample:

Lining Fabric Sample:

Notes:

....
....
....
....
....
....
....
....

Interfacing Sample:

How was it ?

◯ ◯ ◯ ◯
Bad Mhh,Ok Liked it Loved it!

Difficulty: ◯ ◯ ◯ ◯

Will I make it again ? ☐ Yes ☐ No

What went well:

....
....
....
....
....
....

What was difficult:

....
....
....
....
....
....

Changes I made to the original pattern:

Notes to my future self:

....
....
....
....
....
....

Project Name:

Start Date:

Sewing Pattern:

End Date:

Supplies

- [ ] ....
- [ ] ....
- [ ] ....
- [ ] ....
- [ ] ....
- [ ] ....
- [ ] ....
- [ ] ....

Sketch:

Thread Used:

Needle Used:

Sewing Machine Settings:
Stitch Length:
Stitch Width:
Stitch Tension:

Main Fabric Sample:

Lining Fabric Sample:

Notes:

....

....

....

....

....

....

....

Interfacing Sample:

How was it ?

◯ ◯ ◯ ◯
Bad Mhh,Ok Liked it Loved it!

Difficulty: ◯ ◯ ◯ ◯

Will I make it again ? ☐ Yes ☐ No

What went well:

....
....
....
....
....
....

What was difficult:

....
....
....
....
....
....

Changes I made to the original pattern:

Notes to my future self:

....
....
....
....
....
....

Project Name:

Start Date:

Sewing Pattern:

End Date:

Supplies

- [ ] ....
- [ ] ....
- [ ] ....
- [ ] ....
- [ ] ....
- [ ] ....
- [ ] ....
- [ ] ....
- [ ] ....

Sketch:

Thread Used:

Needle Used:

Sewing Machine Settings:

Stitch Length:

Stitch Width:

Stitch Tension:

Main Fabric Sample:

Lining Fabric Sample:

Notes:

....

....

....

....

....

....

....

Interfacing Sample:

How was it ?

◯ ◯ ◯ ◯
Bad Mhh,Ok Liked it Loved it!

Difficulty: ◯ ◯ ◯ ◯

Will I make it again ? ☐ Yes ☐ No

What went well:

....
....
....
....
....
....
....

What was difficult:

....
....
....
....
....
....
....

Changes I made to the original pattern:

Notes to my future self:

....
....
....
....
....
....

Project Name: _____

Start Date: _____

Sewing Pattern: _____

End Date: _____

Supplies

- [ ] _____
- [ ] _____
- [ ] _____
- [ ] _____
- [ ] _____
- [ ] _____
- [ ] _____
- [ ] _____
- [ ] _____

Sketch:

Thread Used: _____

Needle Used: _____

Sewing Machine Settings:

Stitch Length:

Stitch Width:

Stitch Tension:

Main Fabric Sample: _____

Lining Fabric Sample: _____

Notes:

_____

_____

_____

_____

_____

_____

_____

Interfacing Sample: _____

How was it ?

◯ ◯ ◯ ◯
Bad   Mhh,Ok   Liked it   Loved it!

Difficulty:

◯ ◯ ◯ ◯

Will I make it again ? ☐ Yes ☐ No

What went well:

What was difficult:

Changes I made to the original pattern:

Notes to my future self:

Project Name:

Sewing Pattern:

Start Date:

End Date:

Supplies

- ☐ ....
- ☐ ....
- ☐ ....
- ☐ ....
- ☐ ....
- ☐ ....
- ☐ ....
- ☐ ....
- ☐ ....

Thread Used:

Needle Used:

Sewing Machine Settings:
Stitch Length:
Stitch Width:
Stitch Tension:

Notes:

....
....
....
....
....
....
....

Sketch:

Main Fabric Sample:

Lining Fabric Sample:

Interfacing Sample:

How was it ?

◯ ◯ ◯ ◯
Bad Mhh,Ok Liked it Loved it!

Difficulty: ◯ ◯ ◯ ◯

Will I make it again ? ☐ Yes ☐ No

What went well:

....
....
....
....
....
....

What was difficult:

....
....
....
....
....
....

Changes I made to the original pattern:

Notes to my future self:

....
....
....
....
....
....

Project Name: _____

Start Date: _____

Sewing Pattern: _____

End Date: _____

Supplies

- [ ] _____
- [ ] _____
- [ ] _____
- [ ] _____
- [ ] _____
- [ ] _____
- [ ] _____
- [ ] _____
- [ ] _____

Sketch:

Thread Used: _____

Needle Used: _____

Sewing Machine Settings:

Stitch Length:

Stitch Width:

Stitch Tension:

Main Fabric Sample: _____

Lining Fabric Sample: _____

Notes:

_____

_____

_____

_____

_____

_____

Interfacing Sample: _____

How was it ?

○ ○ ○ ○
Bad Mhh,Ok Liked it Loved it!

Difficulty: ○ ○ ○ ○

Will I make it again ? ☐ Yes ☐ No

What went well:

....
....
....
....
....
....

What was difficult:

....
....
....
....
....
....

Changes I made to the original pattern:

Notes to my future self:

....
....
....
....
....
....

Project Name:

Start Date:

Sewing Pattern:

End Date:

Supplies

☐ ....
☐ ....
☐ ....
☐ ....
☐ ....
☐ ....
☐ ....
☐ ....
☐ ....

Sketch:

Thread Used:

Needle Used:

Sewing Machine Settings:

Stitch Length:

Stitch Width:

Stitch Tension:

Main Fabric Sample:

Lining Fabric Sample:

Notes:

....
....
....
....
....
....
....
....

Interfacing Sample:

How was it ?

○ ○ ○ ○
Bad Mhh,Ok Liked it Loved it!

Difficulty: ○ ○ ○ ○

Will I make it again ? ☐ Yes ☐ No

What went well:

....
....
....
....
....
....
....

What was difficult:

....
....
....
....
....
....
....

Changes I made to the original pattern:

Notes to my future self:

....
....
....
....
....
....
....
....

Project Name:

Sewing Pattern:

Start Date:

End Date:

Supplies

- ☐ ....
- ☐ ....
- ☐ ....
- ☐ ....
- ☐ ....
- ☐ ....
- ☐ ....
- ☐ ....
- ☐ ....

Sketch:

Thread Used:

Needle Used:

Sewing Machine Settings:
Stitch Length:
Stitch Width:
Stitch Tension:

Main Fabric Sample:

Lining Fabric Sample:

Notes:

....

....

....

....

....

....

....

....

Interfacing Sample:

How was it ?

◯ ◯ ◯ ◯

Bad Mhh,Ok Liked it Loved it!

Difficulty: ◯ ◯ ◯ ◯

Will I make it again ? ☐ Yes ☐ No

What went well:

....

....

....

....

....

....

What was difficult:

....

....

....

....

....

....

Changes I made to the original pattern:

Notes to my future self:

....

....

....

....

....

....

Project Name:

Start Date:

Sewing Pattern:

End Date:

Supplies

- ☐ ....
- ☐ ....
- ☐ ....
- ☐ ....
- ☐ ....
- ☐ ....
- ☐ ....
- ☐ ....
- ☐ ....

Sketch:

Thread Used:

Needle Used:

Sewing Machine Settings:
Stitch Length:
Stitch Width:
Stitch Tension:

Main Fabric Sample:

Lining Fabric Sample:

Notes:

....

....

....

....

....

....

....

Interfacing Sample:

How was it ?

◯ ◯ ◯ ◯
Bad Mhh,Ok Liked it Loved it!

Difficulty: ◯ ◯ ◯ ◯

Will I make it again ? ☐ Yes ☐ No

What went well:

....
....
....
....
....
....

What was difficult:

....
....
....
....
....
....

Changes I made to the original pattern:

Notes to my future self:

....
....
....
....
....
....

Project Name: _____

Sewing Pattern: _____

Start Date: _____

End Date: _____

Supplies

- ☐ ....
- ☐ ....
- ☐ ....
- ☐ ....
- ☐ ....
- ☐ ....
- ☐ ....
- ☐ ....
- ☐ ....

Thread Used: _____

Needle Used: _____

Sewing Machine Settings:

Stitch Length:

Stitch Width:

Stitch Tension:

Notes:

....

....

....

....

....

....

....

....

Sketch:

Main Fabric Sample:

Lining Fabric Sample:

Interfacing Sample:

How was it ?

○ ○ ○ ○
Bad Mhh,Ok Liked it Loved it!

Difficulty: ○ ○ ○ ○

Will I make it again ? ☐ Yes ☐ No

What went well:

....
....
....
....
....
....

What was difficult:

....
....
....
....
....
....

Changes I made to the original pattern:

Notes to my future self:

....
....
....
....
....
....

Project Name: _____

Start Date: _____

Sewing Pattern: _____

End Date: _____

Supplies

- [ ] ....
- [ ] ....
- [ ] ....
- [ ] ....
- [ ] ....
- [ ] ....
- [ ] ....
- [ ] ....
- [ ] ....

Sketch:

Thread Used: _____

Needle Used: _____

Sewing Machine Settings:

Stitch Length:

Stitch Width:

Stitch Tension:

Main Fabric Sample: _____

Lining Fabric Sample: _____

Notes:

....

....

....

....

....

....

....

Interfacing Sample: _____

How was it ?

◯ ◯ ◯ ◯
Bad Mhh,Ok Liked it Loved it!

Difficulty: ◯ ◯ ◯ ◯

Will I make it again ? ☐ Yes ☐ No

What went well:

....
....
....
....
....
....

What was difficult:

....
....
....
....
....
....

Changes I made to the original pattern:

Notes to my future self:

....
....
....
....
....
....

Project Name:

Start Date:

Sewing Pattern:

End Date:

Supplies

- ☐ ....
- ☐ ....
- ☐ ....
- ☐ ....
- ☐ ....
- ☐ ....
- ☐ ....
- ☐ ....
- ☐ ....

Sketch:

Thread Used:

Needle Used:

Sewing Machine Settings:

Stitch Length:

Stitch Width:

Stitch Tension:

Main Fabric Sample:

Lining Fabric Sample:

Notes:

....

....

....

....

....

....

....

....

Interfacing Sample:

How was it ?

◯ ◯ ◯ ◯
Bad   Mhh,Ok Liked it Loved it!

Difficulty: ◯ ◯ ◯ ◯

Will I make it again ? ☐ Yes ☐ No

What went well:

....
....
....
....
....
....

What was difficult:

....
....
....
....
....
....

Changes I made to the original pattern:

Notes to my future self:

....
....
....
....
....
....

Project Name:

Start Date:

Sewing Pattern:

End Date:

Supplies

- ☐ ....
- ☐ ....
- ☐ ....
- ☐ ....
- ☐ ....
- ☐ ....
- ☐ ....
- ☐ ....
- ☐ ....

Sketch:

Thread Used: _____

Needle Used: _____

Sewing Machine Settings:

Stitch Length:

Stitch Width:

Stitch Tension:

Main Fabric Sample:

Lining Fabric Sample:

Notes:

....
....
....
....
....
....
....
....

Interfacing Sample:

How was it ?

○ ○ ○ ○
Bad Mhh,Ok Liked it Loved it!

Difficulty: ○ ○ ○ ○

Will I make it again ? ☐ Yes ☐ No

What went well:

....
....
....
....
....
....

What was difficult:

....
....
....
....
....
....

Changes I made to the original pattern:

Notes to my future self:

....
....
....
....
....
....
....

Project Name:

Start Date:

Sewing Pattern:

End Date:

Supplies

- ☐ ....
- ☐ ....
- ☐ ....
- ☐ ....
- ☐ ....
- ☐ ....
- ☐ ....
- ☐ ....
- ☐ ....

Sketch:

Thread Used:

Needle Used:

Sewing Machine Settings:

Stitch Length:

Stitch Width:

Stitch Tension:

Main Fabric Sample:

Lining Fabric Sample:

Notes:

....

....

....

....

....

....

....

Interfacing Sample:

How was it ?

◯ ◯ ◯ ◯
Bad Mhh,Ok Liked it Loved it!

Difficulty: ◯ ◯ ◯ ◯

Will I make it again ? ☐ Yes ☐ No

What went well:

....

....

....

....

....

....

What was difficult:

....

....

....

....

....

....

Changes I made to the original pattern:

Notes to my future self:

....

....

....

....

....

....

Project Name: _____

Start Date: _____

Sewing Pattern: _____

End Date: _____

Supplies

- ☐ ....
- ☐ ....
- ☐ ....
- ☐ ....
- ☐ ....
- ☐ ....
- ☐ ....
- ☐ ....
- ☐ ....

Sketch:

Thread Used: _____

Needle Used: _____

Sewing Machine Settings:

Stitch Length:

Stitch Width:

Stitch Tension:

Main Fabric Sample: _____

Lining Fabric Sample: _____

Notes:

....
....
....
....
....
....
....
....

Interfacing Sample: _____

How was it ?

○ ○ ○ ○
Bad   Mhh,Ok   Liked it   Loved it!

Difficulty: ○ ○ ○ ○

Will I make it again ? ☐ Yes ☐ No

What went well:

....
....
....
....
....
....
....

What was difficult:

....
....
....
....
....
....
....

Changes I made to the original pattern:

Notes to my future self:

....
....
....
....
....
....
....

Project Name:

Start Date:

Sewing Pattern:

End Date:

Supplies

- [ ] ....
- [ ] ....
- [ ] ....
- [ ] ....
- [ ] ....
- [ ] ....
- [ ] ....
- [ ] ....
- [ ] ....

Sketch:

Thread Used:

Needle Used:

Sewing Machine Settings:

Stitch Length:

Stitch Width:

Stitch Tension:

Main Fabric Sample:

Lining Fabric Sample:

Notes:

....

....

....

....

....

....

....

....

Interfacing Sample:

How was it ?

◯ ◯ ◯ ◯
Bad Mhh,Ok Liked it Loved it!

Difficulty: ◯ ◯ ◯ ◯

Will I make it again ? ☐ Yes ☐ No

What went well:

....
....
....
....
....
....

What was difficult:

....
....
....
....
....
....

Changes I made to the original pattern:

Notes to my future self:

....
....
....
....
....
....

Project Name: _____   Start Date: _____

Sewing Pattern: _____   End Date: _____

Supplies

- ☐ ....
- ☐ ....
- ☐ ....
- ☐ ....
- ☐ ....
- ☐ ....
- ☐ ....
- ☐ ....
- ☐ ....

Sketch:

Thread Used: _____

Needle Used: _____

Sewing Machine Settings:

Stitch Length:

Stitch Width:

Stitch Tension:

Main Fabric Sample:

Lining Fabric Sample:

Notes:

....

....

....

....

....

....

....

....

Interfacing Sample:

How was it ?

◯ ◯ ◯ ◯

Bad   Mhh,Ok   Liked it   Loved it!

Difficulty: ◯ ◯ ◯ ◯

Will I make it again ? ☐ Yes ☐ No

What went well:

....
....
....
....
....
....

What was difficult:

....
....
....
....
....
....

Changes I made to the original pattern:

Notes to my future self:

....
....
....
....
....
....

Project Name:

Start Date:

Sewing Pattern:

End Date:

Supplies

- ☐ ....
- ☐ ....
- ☐ ....
- ☐ ....
- ☐ ....
- ☐ ....
- ☐ ....
- ☐ ....
- ☐ ....

Sketch:

Thread Used:

Needle Used:

Sewing Machine Settings:

Stitch Length:

Stitch Width:

Stitch Tension:

Main Fabric Sample:

Lining Fabric Sample:

Notes:

....

....

....

....

....

....

....

Interfacing Sample:

How was it ?

◯ ◯ ◯ ◯

Bad   Mhh,Ok   Liked it   Loved it!

Difficulty: ◯ ◯ ◯ ◯

Will I make it again ? ☐ Yes ☐ No

What went well:

....
....
....
....
....
....

What was difficult:

....
....
....
....
....
....

Changes I made to the original pattern:

Notes to my future self:

....
....
....
....
....
....

Project Name: _____

Sewing Pattern: _____

Start Date: _____

End Date: _____

Supplies

- ☐ ....
- ☐ ....
- ☐ ....
- ☐ ....
- ☐ ....
- ☐ ....
- ☐ ....
- ☐ ....
- ☐ ....

Sketch:

Thread Used: _____

Needle Used: _____

Sewing Machine Settings:

Stitch Length:

Stitch Width:

Stitch Tension:

Main Fabric Sample:

Lining Fabric Sample:

Notes:

....

....

....

....

....

....

....

....

Interfacing Sample:

How was it ?

○ ○ ○ ○
Bad   Mhh,Ok Liked it Loved it!

Difficulty: ○ ○ ○ ○

Will I make it again ? ☐ Yes ☐ No

What went well:

....
....
....
....
....
....

What was difficult:

....
....
....
....
....
....

Changes I made to the original pattern:

Notes to my future self:

....
....
....
....
....
....

Project Name:

Start Date:

Sewing Pattern:

End Date:

Supplies

- ☐ ....
- ☐ ....
- ☐ ....
- ☐ ....
- ☐ ....
- ☐ ....
- ☐ ....
- ☐ ....
- ☐ ....

Sketch:

Thread Used:

Needle Used:

Sewing Machine Settings:

Stitch Length:

Stitch Width:

Stitch Tension:

Main Fabric Sample:

Lining Fabric Sample:

Notes:

....

....

....

....

....

....

....

....

Interfacing Sample:

How was it ?

◯ ◯ ◯ ◯
Bad Mhh,Ok Liked it Loved it!

Difficulty: ◯ ◯ ◯ ◯

Will I make it again ? ☐ Yes ☐ No

What went well:

....
....
....
....
....
....

What was difficult:

....
....
....
....
....
....

Changes I made to the original pattern:

Notes to my future self:

....
....
....
....
....
....
....

Project Name: _____ Start Date: _____

Sewing Pattern: _____ End Date: _____

Supplies

- ☐ ....
- ☐ ....
- ☐ ....
- ☐ ....
- ☐ ....
- ☐ ....
- ☐ ....
- ☐ ....
- ☐ ....

Sketch:

Thread Used: _____

Needle Used: _____

Sewing Machine Settings:

Stitch Length:

Stitch Width:

Stitch Tension:

Main Fabric Sample: _____

Notes:

....

....

....

....

....

....

....

....

Lining Fabric Sample: _____

Interfacing Sample: _____

How was it ?

○ ○ ○ ○
Bad   Mhh,Ok   Liked it   Loved it!

Difficulty: ○ ○ ○ ○

Will I make it again ? ☐ Yes ☐ No

What went well:

....
....
....
....
....
....
....

What was difficult:

....
....
....
....
....
....
....

Changes I made to the original pattern:

Notes to my future self:

....
....
....
....
....
....
....

Project Name: _____

Sewing Pattern: _____

Start Date: _____

End Date: _____

Supplies

- [ ] ....
- [ ] ....
- [ ] ....
- [ ] ....
- [ ] ....
- [ ] ....
- [ ] ....
- [ ] ....
- [ ] ....

Thread Used: _____

Needle Used: _____

Sewing Machine Settings:

Stitch Length:

Stitch Width:

Stitch Tension:

Notes:

....

....

....

....

....

....

....

....

Sketch:

Main Fabric Sample: _____

Lining Fabric Sample: _____

Interfacing Sample:

How was it ?

◯ ◯ ◯ ◯
Bad Mhh,Ok Liked it Loved it!

Difficulty: ◯ ◯ ◯ ◯

Will I make it again ? ☐ Yes ☐ No

What went well:

....
....
....
....
....
....

What was difficult:

....
....
....
....
....
....

Changes I made to the original pattern:

Notes to my future self:

....
....
....
....
....
....

Project Name: _____

Start Date: _____

Sewing Pattern: _____

End Date: _____

Supplies

- [ ] _____
- [ ] _____
- [ ] _____
- [ ] _____
- [ ] _____
- [ ] _____
- [ ] _____
- [ ] _____
- [ ] _____

Sketch:

Thread Used: _____

Needle Used: _____

Sewing Machine Settings:

Stitch Length:

Stitch Width:

Stitch Tension:

Main Fabric Sample: _____

Lining Fabric Sample: _____

Notes:

_____
_____
_____
_____
_____
_____
_____
_____

Interfacing Sample: _____

How was it ?

◯ ◯ ◯ ◯
Bad Mhh,Ok Liked it Loved it!

Difficulty: ◯ ◯ ◯ ◯

Will I make it again ? ☐ Yes ☐ No

What went well:

....
....
....
....
....
....
....

What was difficult:

....
....
....
....
....
....
....

Changes I made to the original pattern:

Notes to my future self:

....
....
....
....
....
....
....

Project Name: _____

Start Date: _____

Sewing Pattern: _____

End Date: _____

Supplies

- ☐ ....
- ☐ ....
- ☐ ....
- ☐ ....
- ☐ ....
- ☐ ....
- ☐ ....
- ☐ ....
- ☐ ....

Thread Used: _____

Needle Used: _____

Sewing Machine Settings:

Stitch Length:

Stitch Width:

Stitch Tension:

Notes:

....
....
....
....
....
....
....
....

Sketch:

Main Fabric Sample:

Lining Fabric Sample:

Interfacing Sample:

How was it ?

◯ ◯ ◯ ◯
Bad Mhh,Ok Liked it Loved it!

Difficulty: ◯ ◯ ◯ ◯

Will I make it again ? ☐ Yes ☐ No

What went well:

What was difficult:

Changes I made to the original pattern:

Notes to my future self:

Project Name:

Sewing Pattern:

Start Date:

End Date:

Supplies

- [ ] ....
- [ ] ....
- [ ] ....
- [ ] ....
- [ ] ....
- [ ] ....
- [ ] ....
- [ ] ....
- [ ] ....

Sketch:

Thread Used:

Needle Used:

Sewing Machine Settings:

Stitch Length:

Stitch Width:

Stitch Tension:

Main Fabric Sample:

Lining Fabric Sample:

Interfacing Sample:

Notes:

....

....

....

....

....

....

....

How was it ?

◯ ◯ ◯ ◯
Bad Mhh,Ok Liked it Loved it!

Difficulty: ◯ ◯ ◯ ◯

Will I make it again ? ☐ Yes ☐ No

What went well:

What was difficult:

Changes I made to the original pattern:

Notes to my future self:

Project Name: _____

Start Date: _____

Sewing Pattern: _____

End Date: _____

Supplies

- [ ] ....
- [ ] ....
- [ ] ....
- [ ] ....
- [ ] ....
- [ ] ....
- [ ] ....
- [ ] ....
- [ ] ....

Sketch:

Thread Used: _____

Needle Used: _____

Sewing Machine Settings:

Stitch Length:

Stitch Width:

Stitch Tension:

Main Fabric Sample:

Lining Fabric Sample:

Notes:

....
....
....
....
....
....
....
....

Interfacing Sample:

How was it ?

○ ○ ○ ○
Bad   Mhh,Ok   Liked it   Loved it!

Difficulty: ○ ○ ○ ○

Will I make it again ? ☐ Yes ☐ No

What went well:

....
....
....
....
....
....

What was difficult:

....
....
....
....
....
....

Changes I made to the original pattern:

Notes to my future self:

....
....
....
....
....
....

Project Name:

Sewing Pattern:

Start Date:

End Date:

Supplies

- [ ] ....
- [ ] ....
- [ ] ....
- [ ] ....
- [ ] ....
- [ ] ....
- [ ] ....
- [ ] ....
- [ ] ....

Thread Used:

Needle Used:

Sewing Machine Settings:

Stitch Length:

Stitch Width:

Stitch Tension:

Notes:

....

....

....

....

....

....

....

....

Sketch:

Main Fabric Sample:

Lining Fabric Sample:

Interfacing Sample:

How was it ?

○ ○ ○ ○
Bad   Mhh,Ok   Liked it   Loved it!

Difficulty: ○ ○ ○ ○

Will I make it again ? ☐ Yes ☐ No

What went well:

....
....
....
....
....
....
....

What was difficult:

....
....
....
....
....
....
....

Changes I made to the original pattern:

Notes to my future self:

....
....
....
....
....
....
....
....

Project Name: _____   Start Date: _____

Sewing Pattern: _____   End Date: _____

Supplies

- ☐ ....
- ☐ ....
- ☐ ....
- ☐ ....
- ☐ ....
- ☐ ....
- ☐ ....
- ☐ ....
- ☐ ....

Thread Used: _____

Needle Used: _____

Sewing Machine Settings:
Stitch Length:
Stitch Width:
Stitch Tension:

Notes:

....
....
....
....
....
....
....
....

Sketch:

Main Fabric Sample: _____

Lining Fabric Sample: _____

Interfacing Sample: _____

How was it ?

◯ ◯ ◯ ◯
Bad Mhh,Ok Liked it Loved it!

Difficulty: ◯ ◯ ◯ ◯

Will I make it again ? ☐ Yes ☐ No

What went well:

What was difficult:

Changes I made to the original pattern:

Notes to my future self:

Project Name:

Start Date:

Sewing Pattern:

End Date:

Supplies

- [ ] ....
- [ ] ....
- [ ] ....
- [ ] ....
- [ ] ....
- [ ] ....
- [ ] ....
- [ ] ....
- [ ] ....

Sketch:

Thread Used:

Needle Used:

Sewing Machine Settings:

Stitch Length:

Stitch Width:

Stitch Tension:

Main Fabric Sample:

Notes:

....
....
....
....
....
....
....

Lining Fabric Sample:

Interfacing Sample:

How was it ?

◯ ◯ ◯ ◯
Bad Mhh,Ok Liked it Loved it!

Difficulty: ◯ ◯ ◯ ◯

Will I make it again ? ☐ Yes ☐ No

What went well:

....
....
....
....
....
....
....

What was difficult:

....
....
....
....
....
....
....

Changes I made to the original pattern:

Notes to my future self:

....
....
....
....
....
....
....

Project Name:

Start Date:

Sewing Pattern:

End Date:

Supplies

- ☐ ....
- ☐ ....
- ☐ ....
- ☐ ....
- ☐ ....
- ☐ ....
- ☐ ....
- ☐ ....
- ☐ ....

Sketch:

Thread Used:

Needle Used:

Sewing Machine Settings:
Stitch Length:
Stitch Width:
Stitch Tension:

Main Fabric Sample:

Lining Fabric Sample:

Notes:

....
....
....
....
....
....
....
....

Interfacing Sample:

How was it ?

○ ○ ○ ○
Bad Mhh,Ok Liked it Loved it!

Difficulty: ○ ○ ○ ○

Will I make it again ? ☐ Yes ☐ No

What went well:

....
....
....
....
....
....

What was difficult:

....
....
....
....
....
....

Changes I made to the original pattern:

Notes to my future self:

....
....
....
....
....
....

Project Name: _____

Start Date: _____

Sewing Pattern: _____

End Date: _____

Supplies

- [ ] ....
- [ ] ....
- [ ] ....
- [ ] ....
- [ ] ....
- [ ] ....
- [ ] ....
- [ ] ....
- [ ] ....

Thread Used: _____

Needle Used: _____

Sewing Machine Settings:

Stitch Length:

Stitch Width:

Stitch Tension:

Notes:

....
....
....
....
....
....
....
....

Sketch:

Main Fabric Sample:

Lining Fabric Sample:

Interfacing Sample:

How was it ?

◯ ◯ ◯ ◯
Bad Mhh,Ok Liked it Loved it!

Difficulty: ◯ ◯ ◯ ◯

Will I make it again ? ☐ Yes ☐ No

What went well:

What was difficult:

Changes I made to the original pattern:

Notes to my future self:

Project Name: _____

Start Date: _____

Sewing Pattern: _____

End Date: _____

Supplies

- [ ] ....
- [ ] ....
- [ ] ....
- [ ] ....
- [ ] ....
- [ ] ....
- [ ] ....
- [ ] ....
- [ ] ....

Sketch:

Thread Used: _____

Needle Used: _____

Sewing Machine Settings:

Stitch Length:

Stitch Width:

Stitch Tension:

Main Fabric Sample:

Lining Fabric Sample:

Notes:

....
....
....
....
....
....
....

Interfacing Sample:

How was it ?

◯ ◯ ◯ ◯
Bad   Mhh,Ok Liked it Loved it!

Difficulty: ◯ ◯ ◯ ◯

Will I make it again ? ☐ Yes ☐ No

What went well:

....
....
....
....
....
....

What was difficult:

....
....
....
....
....
....

Changes I made to the original pattern:

Notes to my future self:

....
....
....
....
....
....

Project Name:

Start Date:

Sewing Pattern:

End Date:

Supplies

- ☐ ....
- ☐ ....
- ☐ ....
- ☐ ....
- ☐ ....
- ☐ ....
- ☐ ....
- ☐ ....
- ☐ ....

Sketch:

Thread Used:

Needle Used:

Sewing Machine Settings:

Stitch Length:

Stitch Width:

Stitch Tension:

Main Fabric Sample:

Lining Fabric Sample:

Notes:

....

....

....

....

....

....

....

....

Interfacing Sample:

How was it ?

◯ ◯ ◯ ◯

Bad   Mhh,Ok   Liked it   Loved it!

Difficulty: ◯ ◯ ◯ ◯

Will I make it again ? ☐ Yes ☐ No

What went well:

....
....
....
....
....
....

What was difficult:

....
....
....
....
....
....

Changes I made to the original pattern:

Notes to my future self:

....
....
....
....
....
....

Project Name:

Start Date:

Sewing Pattern:

End Date:

Supplies

- ☐ ....
- ☐ ....
- ☐ ....
- ☐ ....
- ☐ ....
- ☐ ....
- ☐ ....
- ☐ ....
- ☐ ....

Sketch:

Thread Used:

Needle Used:

Sewing Machine Settings:

Stitch Length:

Stitch Width:

Stitch Tension:

Main Fabric Sample:

Lining Fabric Sample:

Notes:

....

....

....

....

....

....

....

....

Interfacing Sample:

How was it ?

○ ○ ○ ○
Bad Mhh,Ok Liked it Loved it!

Difficulty: ○ ○ ○ ○

Will I make it again ? ☐ Yes ☐ No

What went well:

....
....
....
....
....
....
....

What was difficult:

....
....
....
....
....
....
....

Changes I made to the original pattern:

Notes to my future self:

....
....
....
....
....
....
....
....

Project Name: _____

Start Date: _____

Sewing Pattern: _____

End Date: _____

Supplies

- ☐ ....
- ☐ ....
- ☐ ....
- ☐ ....
- ☐ ....
- ☐ ....
- ☐ ....
- ☐ ....
- ☐ ....

Sketch: _____

Thread Used: _____

Needle Used: _____

Sewing Machine Settings:

Stitch Length:

Stitch Width:

Stitch Tension:

Main Fabric Sample: _____

Lining Fabric Sample: _____

Notes:

....
....
....
....
....
....
....
....

Interfacing Sample: _____

How was it ?

◯ ◯ ◯ ◯
Bad Mhh,Ok Liked it Loved it!

Difficulty: ◯ ◯ ◯ ◯

Will I make it again ? ☐ Yes ☐ No

What went well:

....
....
....
....
....
....
....

What was difficult:

....
....
....
....
....
....
....

Changes I made to the original pattern:

Notes to my future self:

....
....
....
....
....
....
....

Project Name: _____   Start Date: _____

Sewing Pattern: _____   End Date: _____

Supplies

- ☐ ....
- ☐ ....
- ☐ ....
- ☐ ....
- ☐ ....
- ☐ ....
- ☐ ....
- ☐ ....
- ☐ ....

Thread Used: _____

Needle Used: _____

Sewing Machine Settings:

Stitch Length:

Stitch Width:

Stitch Tension:

Notes:

....

....

....

....

....

....

....

Sketch:

Main Fabric Sample:

Lining Fabric Sample:

Interfacing Sample:

How was it ?

◯ ◯ ◯ ◯
Bad   Mhh,Ok   Liked it   Loved it!

Difficulty: ◯ ◯ ◯ ◯

Will I make it again ? ☐ Yes ☐ No

What went well:

What was difficult:

Changes I made to the original pattern:

Notes to my future self:

Project Name: _____

Sewing Pattern: _____

Start Date: _____

End Date: _____

Supplies

- ☐ ....
- ☐ ....
- ☐ ....
- ☐ ....
- ☐ ....
- ☐ ....
- ☐ ....
- ☐ ....
- ☐ ....

Thread Used: _____

Needle Used: _____

Sewing Machine Settings:

Stitch Length:

Stitch Width:

Stitch Tension:

Notes:

....
....
....
....
....
....
....
....

Sketch:

Main Fabric Sample: _____

Lining Fabric Sample:

Interfacing Sample:

How was it ?

◯ ◯ ◯ ◯
Bad Mhh,Ok Liked it Loved it!

Difficulty: ◯ ◯ ◯ ◯

Will I make it again ? ☐ Yes ☐ No

What went well:

....
....
....
....
....
....
....

What was difficult:

....
....
....
....
....
....
....

Changes I made to the original pattern:

Notes to my future self:

....
....
....
....
....
....
....

Made in the USA
Las Vegas, NV
27 December 2023

83588424R00057